THE BROONS

Diary 2018

Week-to-view Diary

Vital Dates for 2018

Quizzes and Recipes

Broons Wisdom

Fun from the Happy Family that
Makes Every Family Happy

BLACK & WHITE PUBLISHING

Important Information

This diary belongs tae:
_____

If found, please return tae:
_____

_____

_____

Tel:
_____

In an emergency, please contact:
_____

_____

Mobile:
_____

Home phone: _____ Work phone: _____

Email: _____ Work email: _____

Notes

_____

_____

_____

_____

_____

_____

_____

_____

_____

_____

_____

_____

_____

2018

January

M	T	W	T	F	S	S
1	2	3	4	5	6	7
8	9	10	11	12	13	14
15	16	17	18	19	20	21
22	23	24	25	26	27	28
29	30	31				

February

M	T	W	T	F	S	S
			1	2	3	4
5	6	7	8	9	10	11
12	13	14	15	16	17	18
19	20	21	22	23	24	25
26	27	28				

March

M	T	W	T	F	S	S
			1	2	3	4
5	6	7	8	9	10	11
12	13	14	15	16	17	18
19	20	21	22	23	24	25
26	27	28	29	30	31	

April

M	T	W	T	F	S	S
30						1
2	3	4	5	6	7	8
9	10	11	12	13	14	15
16	17	18	19	20	21	22
23	24	25	26	27	28	29

May

M	T	W	T	F	S	S
	1	2	3	4	5	6
7	8	9	10	11	12	13
14	15	16	17	18	19	20
21	22	23	24	25	26	27
28	29	30	31			

June

M	T	W	T	F	S	S
				1	2	3
4	5	6	7	8	9	10
11	12	13	14	15	16	17
18	19	20	21	22	23	24
25	26	27	28	29	30	

July

M	T	W	T	F	S	S
30	31					1
2	3	4	5	6	7	8
9	10	11	12	13	14	15
16	17	18	19	20	21	22
23	24	25	26	27	28	29

August

M	T	W	T	F	S	S
		1	2	3	4	5
6	7	8	9	10	11	12
13	14	15	16	17	18	19
20	21	22	23	24	25	26
27	28	29	30	31		

September

M	T	W	T	F	S	S
					1	2
3	4	5	6	7	8	9
10	11	12	13	14	15	16
17	18	19	20	21	22	23
24	25	26	27	28	29	30

October

M	T	W	T	F	S	S
1	2	3	4	5	6	7
8	9	10	11	12	13	14
15	16	17	18	19	20	21
22	23	24	25	26	27	28
29	30	31				

November

M	T	W	T	F	S	S
			1	2	3	4
5	6	7	8	9	10	11
12	13	14	15	16	17	18
19	20	21	22	23	24	25
26	27	28	29	30		

December

M	T	W	T	F	S	S
31					1	2
3	4	5	6	7	8	9
10	11	12	13	14	15	16
17	18	19	20	21	22	23
24	25	26	27	28	29	30

Notable Dates

JANUARY

Monday 1st	New Year's Day, holiday
Tuesday 2nd	Holiday (Scot)
Friday 5th	Twelfth Night
Saturday 6th	Epiphany
Sunday 14th	Makar Sankranti
Monday 15th	Martin Luther King, Jr. Day, holiday (US)
Monday 22nd	Vasant Panchami
Thursday 25th	Burns Night
Friday 26th	Australia Day, holiday (Aus)
Saturday 27th	Holocaust Memorial Day (UK)

FEBRUARY

Friday 2nd	Groundhog Day (Can, US)
Tuesday 6th	Waitangi Day, holiday (NZ)
Tuesday 13th	Shrove Tuesday
Wednesday 14th	St Valentine's Day
	Ash Wednesday
Friday 16th	Chinese New Year (Year of the Dog)
Monday 19th	Presidents' Day, holiday (US)
Wednesday 28th	Purim begins at sunset

MARCH

Thursday 1st	St. David's Day
	Holi begins at sunset
Sunday 11th	Mother's Day (UK)
	Daylight Saving Time begins (US, Can)
Monday 12th	Commonwealth Day
Saturday 17th	St. Patrick's Day
Sunday 25th	British Summer Time begins
	Rama Navami
Friday 30th	Good Friday
	Passover begins at sunset
Saturday 31st	Hanuman Jayanti

APRIL

Sunday 1st	Easter Sunday
	April Fool's Day
Monday 2nd	Easter Monday
Friday 6th	Tartan Day (Can, US)
Saturday 7th	Passover ends at sunset
Monday 9th	Vimy Ridge Day (Can)
Wednesday 11th	Yom HaShoah begins at sunset
Monday 16th	Emancipation Day
Monday 23rd	St. George's Day
Wednesday 25th	Anzac Day

MAY

Tuesday 1st	May Day
Thursday 10th	Ascension Day
Sunday 13th	Mother's Day (Aus, Can, NZ, US)
Tuesday 15th	Ramadan begins at sunset
Saturday 19th	Shavuot begins at sunset
Sunday 20th	Pentecost
Monday 21st	Victoria Day
	Shavuot ends at sunset
Saturday 26th	National Sorry Day (Aus)
Sunday 27th	Trinity Sunday
Monday 28th	Spring Bank Holiday (UK, R of I)
	Memorial Day (US)
Thursday 31st	Corpus Christi

JUNE

Sunday 10th	Laylat al-Qadr begins at sunset
Thursday 14th	Ramadan ends at sunset
	Eid al-Fitr begins at sunset
Sunday 17th	Father's Day (UK, US, Can, R of I)
Thursday 21st	Summer Solstice
	National Aboriginal Day (Can)
Sunday 24th	St. John the Baptist Day

JULY

Sunday 1st	Canada Day
Wednesday 4th	Independence Day
Thursday 12th	Battle of the Boyne
Sunday 15th	St. Swithin's Day
Saturday 21st	Tisha B'Av begins at sunset

AUGUST

Monday 6th	Civic Day (Can)
Tuesday 21st	Eid al-Adha begins at sunset
Saturday 25th	Eid al-Adha ends at sunset
Monday 27th	Summer Bank Holiday (UK)

SEPTEMBER

Sunday 2nd	Krishna Janmashtami
	Father's Day (Aus, NZ)
Monday 3rd	Labor Day (US)
Sunday 9th	Rosh Hashanah begins at sunset
Monday 10th	Muharram begins at sunset
Tuesday 11th	Rosh Hashanah ends at sunset
Wednesday 12th	Ganesh Chaturthi begins
Tuesday 18th	Yom Kippur begins at sunset
Friday 21st	International Day of Peace (United Nations)
Sunday 23rd	Ganesh Chaturthi ends
	Sukkot begins at sunset
Sunday 30th	New Zealand Daylight Saving Time begins
	Sukkot ends at sunset

OCTOBER

Sunday 7th	Australian Daylight Saving Time begins
Monday 8th	Columbus Day (US)
Tuesday 9th	Muharram ends at sunset
	Navratri begins
Wednesday 10th	World Porridge Day
Wednesday 17th	Navratri ends
Sunday 28th	British Summer Time ends
Wednesday 31st	Halloween

NOVEMBER

Thursday 1st	All Saints' Day
Friday 2nd	All Souls' Day
Sunday 4th	Daylight Saving Time ends (US, Can)
Monday 5th	Guy Fawkes Night (UK)
Wednesday 7th	Diwali begins
Sunday 11th	Remembrance Sunday (UK)
	Veterans Day (US)
	Diwali ends
Tuesday 13th	Robert Louis Stevenson Day
Thursday 22nd	Thanksgiving Day (US)
Friday 30th	St. Andrew's Day

DECEMBER

Sunday 2nd	Advent Sunday
	Hanukkah begins at sunset
Monday 10th	Human Rights Day
	Hanukkah ends at sunset
Friday 21st	Winter Solstice
Monday 24th	Christmas Eve
Tuesday 25th	Christmas Day, holiday
Wednesday 26th	Boxing Day, holiday
Monday 31st	Hogmanay (New Year's Eve)

Clothing Sizes

WOMEN'S CLOTHING SIZE

UK	4	6	8	10	12	14	16	18	20	22	24
US	0	2	4	6	8	10	12	14	16	18	20
EU	34	36	38	40	42	44	46	48	50	52	54

GIRLS' DRESSES AND COATS

UK	3	5	7	9	11	13	15	17
US	1	3	5	7	9	11	13	15
EU	28	30	32	34	36	38	40	42

MEN'S SUITS, JUMPERS AND COATS

UK/US	38	40	42	44	46	48	50	52	54
EU	48	50	52	54	56	58	60	62	64

MEN'S SHIRTS

	S	M	L	XL	XXL	3XL	4XL
UK/US	14-14½	15-15½	16-16½	17-17½	18-18½	19-19½	20-20½
EU	36	38-40	42-44	46-48	50-52	54-56	58-60

HAT SIZES

UK	$6\frac{3}{8}$	$6\frac{1}{2}$	$6\frac{5}{8}$	$6\frac{3}{4}$	$6\frac{7}{8}$	7	$7\frac{1}{8}$	$7\frac{1}{4}$	$7\frac{3}{8}$	$7\frac{1}{2}$	$7\frac{5}{8}$
US	$6\frac{1}{2}$	$6\frac{5}{8}$	$6\frac{3}{4}$	$6\frac{7}{8}$	7	$7\frac{1}{8}$	$7\frac{1}{4}$	$7\frac{3}{8}$	$7\frac{1}{2}$	$7\frac{5}{8}$	$7\frac{3}{4}$
Inches	$20\frac{1}{2}$	$20\frac{7}{8}$	$21\frac{1}{4}$	$21\frac{5}{8}$	22	$22\frac{1}{2}$	$22\frac{7}{8}$	$23\frac{1}{4}$	$23\frac{5}{8}$	24	$24\frac{1}{2}$
Centimetres	52	53	54	55	56	57	58	59	60	61	62

& Conversions

WOMEN'S SHOES

UK	2	2.5	3	3.5	4	4.5	5	5.5	6	6.5	7	7.5	8
US	4.5	5	5.5	6	6.5	7	7.5	8	8.5	9	9.5	10	10.5
EU	34	35	35.5	36	37	37.5	38	38.5	39	39.5	40	41	42

MEN'S SHOES

UK	5	5.5	6	6.5	7	7.5	8	8.5	9	9.5	10	10.5	11	11.5	12
US	5.5	6	6.5	7	7.5	8	8.5	9	9.5	10	10.5	11	11.5	12	12.5
EU	38	38.7	39.3	40	40.5	41	42	42.5	43	44	44.5	45	46	46.5	47

GIRLS' SHOES

UK	8	8.5	9	9.5	10	10.5	11	11.5	12	12.5	13	13.5	1	1.5	2	2.5
US	8.5	9	9.5	10	10.5	11	11.5	12	13.5	1	1.5	2	2.5	3	3.5	4
EU	26	26.5	27	27.5	28	28.5	29	30	30.5	31	31.5	32.2	33	33.5	34	35

BOYS' SHOES

UK	11	11.5	12	12.5	13	13.5	1	1.5	2	2.5	3	3.5	4	4.5
US	11.5	12	12.5	13	13.5	1	1.5	2	2.5	3	3.5	4	4.5	5
EU	29	29.7	30.5	31	31.5	33	33.5	34	34.7	35	35.5	36	37	37.5

January

The aulder Broons are tired oot
From New Year song an' dance.
The bairns were sent tae bed nae dout,
So noo they tak their chance!

January

1 Monday

New Year's Day, holiday

2 Tuesday

Holiday (Scot)

3 Wednesday

January

4 Thursday

5 Friday

Twelfth Night

6 Saturday

Epiphany

7 Sunday

Wk	M	T	W	T	F	S	S
1	1	2	3	4	5	6	7
2	8	9	10	11	12	13	14
3	15	16	17	18	19	20	21
4	22	23	24	25	26	27	28
5	29	30	31				

January

8 Monday

9 Tuesday

10 Wednesday

January

11 Thursday

12 Friday

13 Saturday

14 Sunday

Makar Sankranti

Wk	M	T	W	T	F	S	S
1	1	2	3	4	5	6	7
2	8	9	10	11	12	13	14
3	15	16	17	18	19	20	21
4	22	23	24	25	26	27	28
5	29	30	31				

January

15 Monday

Martin Luther King, Jr. Day, holiday (US)

16 Tuesday

17 Wednesday

January

18 Thursday

19 Friday

20 Saturday

21 Sunday

Wk	M	T	W	T	F	S	S
1	1	2	3	4	5	6	7
2	8	9	10	11	12	13	14
3	15	16	17	18	19	20	21
4	22	23	24	25	26	27	28
5	29	30	31				

January

22 Monday

Vasant Panchami

23 Tuesday

24 Wednesday

January

25 Thursday

...ns Night

_____

26 Friday

Australia Day, holiday (Aus)

_____

27 Saturday

Holocaust Memorial Day (UK)

_____

28 Sunday

_____

Wk	M	T	W	T	F	S	S
1	1	2	3	4	5	6	7
2	8	9	10	11	12	13	14
3	15	16	17	18	19	20	21
4	22	23	24	25	26	27	28
5	29	30	31				

January

29 Monday

30 Tuesday

31 Wednesday

February

Oor Daphne's got a Valentine.
He's wee and kinda bandy
The family think that he's just fine –
The milk will come in handy!

To a Wee Lamb
The Bairn's Burns Style Tribute to Her Dolly

Wee, sleepy, cuddly, little lamb,
Oh, how ye luv yer braw wee pram.
How can ye doze awa' sae calmly
Whilst thae twins prattle?
And ither members o' the family
Clump roond like cattle?

There's Hen an' Joe's o'er loud opinions
And Maw so noisy choppin' ingins
And Gran'paw yelpin' wi' his bunions,
But you don't waken.
Wee pet, my dearest young companion
Ye tak SOME shakin'!

February

1 Thursday

_____

_____

_____

_____

_____

_____

_____

_____

_____

_____

_____

_____

_____

_____

_____

_____

_____

_____

_____

_____

_____

_____

_____

_____

_____

_____

2 Friday

Groundhog Day (Can, US)

_____

_____

_____

_____

_____

_____

_____

_____

_____

_____

_____

_____

_____

_____

_____

_____

_____

_____

_____

_____

_____

_____

_____

_____

_____

3 Saturday

_____

_____

_____

_____

_____

_____

_____

_____

_____

4 Sunday

_____

_____

_____

_____

_____

_____

_____

_____

_____

_____

_____

Wk	M	T	W	T	F	S	S
5				1	2	3	4
6	5	6	7	8	9	10	11
7	12	13	14	15	16	17	18
8	19	20	21	22	23	24	25
9	26	27	28				

February

5 Monday

_____
_____
_____
_____
_____
_____
_____
_____
_____
_____
_____
_____
_____
_____
_____
_____
_____
_____
_____
_____
_____
_____
_____
_____
_____
_____
_____
_____

6 Tuesday

Waitangi Day, holiday (NZ)
_____
_____
_____
_____
_____
_____
_____
_____
_____
_____
_____
_____
_____
_____
_____
_____
_____
_____
_____
_____
_____
_____
_____
_____
_____
_____
_____
_____

7 Wednesday

_____
_____
_____
_____
_____
_____
_____
_____
_____
_____
_____
_____
_____
_____
_____
_____
_____
_____
_____
_____
_____
_____
_____
_____
_____
_____
_____
_____

February

8 Thursday

_____
_____
_____
_____
_____
_____
_____
_____
_____
_____
_____
_____
_____
_____
_____
_____
_____
_____
_____
_____
_____
_____
_____
_____
_____
_____

9 Friday

_____
_____
_____
_____
_____
_____
_____
_____
_____
_____
_____
_____
_____
_____
_____
_____
_____
_____
_____
_____
_____
_____
_____
_____
_____
_____

10 Saturday

_____
_____
_____
_____
_____
_____
_____
_____
_____

11 Sunday

_____
_____
_____
_____
_____
_____
_____
_____
_____
_____
_____

Wk	M	T	W	T	F	S	S
5				1	2	3	4
6	5	6	7	8	9	10	11
7	12	13	14	15	16	17	18
8	19	20	21	22	23	24	25
9	26	27	28				

February

12 Monday

_____
_____
_____
_____
_____
_____
_____
_____
_____
_____
_____
_____
_____
_____
_____
_____
_____
_____
_____
_____
_____
_____
_____

13 Tuesday

Shrove Tuesday

_____
_____
_____
_____
_____
_____
_____
_____
_____
_____
_____
_____
_____
_____
_____
_____
_____
_____
_____
_____
_____
_____

14 Wednesday

St Valentine's Day

Ash Wednesday

_____
_____
_____
_____
_____
_____
_____
_____
_____
_____
_____
_____
_____
_____
_____
_____
_____
_____
_____
_____
_____

February

15 Thursday

_____
_____
_____
_____
_____
_____
_____
_____
_____
_____
_____
_____
_____
_____
_____
_____
_____
_____
_____
_____
_____
_____
_____
_____
_____

16 Friday

Chinese New Year (Year of the Dog)

_____
_____
_____
_____
_____
_____
_____
_____
_____
_____
_____
_____
_____
_____
_____
_____
_____
_____
_____
_____
_____
_____
_____

17 Saturday

_____
_____
_____
_____
_____
_____
_____

18 Sunday

_____
_____
_____
_____
_____
_____
_____
_____
_____
_____

Wk	M	T	W	T	F	S	S
5				1	2	3	4
6	5	6	7	8	9	10	11
7	12	13	14	15	16	17	18
8	19	20	21	22	23	24	25
9	26	27	28				

February

19 Monday

Presidents' Day, holiday (US)

20 Tuesday

21 Wednesday

February

22 Thursday

23 Friday

24 Saturday

25 Sunday

Wk	M	T	W	T	F	S	S
5				1	2	3	4
6	5	6	7	8	9	10	11
7	12	13	14	15	16	17	18
8	19	20	21	22	23	24	25
9	26	27	28				

February

26 Monday

_____
_____
_____
_____
_____
_____
_____
_____
_____
_____
_____
_____
_____
_____
_____
_____
_____
_____
_____
_____
_____
_____
_____
_____
_____

27 Tuesday

_____
_____
_____
_____
_____
_____
_____
_____
_____
_____
_____
_____
_____
_____
_____
_____
_____
_____
_____
_____
_____
_____
_____
_____
_____

28 Wednesday

Purim begins at sunset
_____
_____
_____
_____
_____
_____
_____
_____
_____
_____
_____
_____
_____
_____
_____
_____
_____
_____
_____
_____
_____
_____
_____
_____
_____

March

Gran'paw's planted oot his seed.
He winks and looks all-knowing.
No greenhouse does this auld lad need –
Look whaur he does his growing!

Maw's Cock-A-Leekie Soup

Here's a grand way tae use up leftover chicken . . . no' that there's ever that much left over in oor hoose!

YE'LL NEED:
(Feeds 8)
4 leeks, washed and sliced
2 carrots, peeled and cut intae chunks
2 sticks of celery, chopped
40g of long grain rice
1.5 litres of water
100 ml of chicken stock or a couple o' chicken stock cubes in 100 ml o' water
1 large tbsp of chopped parsley
200g of chopped leftover chicken
Ground black pepper to taste

METHOD:
1. Pit the vegetables, water and stock (or cubes) in a large saucepan. Bring tae the boil then reduce the heat and simmer for aboot ten minutes.
2. Add the rice and continue tae cook for anither fifteen minutes.
3. Add the parsley and cooked chicken and gie it aboot anither five minutes.
4. Add pepper tae taste and Bob's yer uncle. Just the job on a cauld day!

March

1 Thursday

David's Day

i begins at sunset

---

2 Friday

---

3 Saturday

---

4 Sunday

Wk	M	T	W	T	F	S	S
9				1	2	3	4
10	5	6	7	8	9	10	11
11	12	13	14	15	16	17	18
12	19	20	21	22	23	24	25
13	26	27	28	29	30	31	

March

5 Monday

6 Tuesday

7 Wednesday

March

8 Thursday

9 Friday

10 Saturday

11 Sunday

Mother's Day (UK)

Daylight Saving Time begins (US, Can)

Wk	M	T	W	T	F	S	S
9				1	2	3	4
10	5	6	7	8	9	10	11
11	12	13	14	15	16	17	18
12	19	20	21	22	23	24	25
13	26	27	28	29	30	31	

March

12 Monday

Commonwealth Day

13 Tuesday

14 Wednesday

March

15 Thursday

_____
_____
_____
_____
_____
_____
_____
_____
_____
_____
_____
_____
_____
_____
_____
_____
_____
_____
_____
_____
_____
_____
_____
_____
_____
_____
_____
_____
_____

16 Friday

_____
_____
_____
_____
_____
_____
_____
_____
_____
_____
_____
_____
_____
_____
_____
_____
_____
_____
_____
_____
_____
_____
_____
_____
_____
_____
_____
_____
_____

17 Saturday

St. Patrick's Day

_____
_____
_____
_____
_____
_____
_____
_____

18 Sunday

_____
_____
_____
_____
_____
_____
_____
_____
_____
_____
_____

Wk	M	T	W	T	F	S	S
9				1	2	3	4
10	5	6	7	8	9	10	11
11	12	13	14	15	16	17	18
12	19	20	21	22	23	24	25
13	26	27	28	29	30	31	

March

19 Monday

20 Tuesday

21 Wednesday

March

22 Thursday

23 Friday

24 Saturday

25 Sunday

British Summer Time begins

Rama Navami

Wk	M	T	W	T	F	S	S
9				1	2	3	4
10	5	6	7	8	9	10	11
11	12	13	14	15	16	17	18
12	19	20	21	22	23	24	25
13	26	27	28	29	30	31	

March

26 Monday   **27** Tuesday   **28** Wednesday

April

"Boost tulip bulbs beneath the bed,"
Says Paw, "Whit could go wrang?"
But, michty, does his Face look red,
When he leaves the plants o'er lang!

SCOTTISH INVENTIONS

THE TELEPHONE – first patented in 1876 by Alexander Graham Bell (1847–1922) from Edinburgh.

March / April

29 Thursday

30 Friday

Good Friday

Passover begins at sunset

31 Saturday

Hanuman Jayanti

1 Sunday

Easter Sunday

April Fool's Day

Wk	M	T	W	T	F	S	S
13							1
14	2	3	4	5	6	7	8
15	9	10	11	12	13	14	15
16	16	17	18	19	20	21	22
17	23	24	25	26	27	28	29
18	30						

April

2 Monday

Easter Monday

3 Tuesday

4 Wednesday

April

5 Thursday

_____
_____
_____
_____
_____
_____
_____
_____
_____
_____
_____
_____
_____
_____
_____
_____
_____
_____
_____
_____
_____
_____
_____
_____
_____
_____
_____

6 Friday

Tartan Day (Can, US)

_____
_____
_____
_____
_____
_____
_____
_____
_____
_____
_____
_____
_____
_____
_____
_____
_____
_____
_____
_____
_____
_____
_____
_____
_____
_____

7 Saturday

Passover ends at sunset

_____
_____
_____
_____
_____
_____
_____
_____

8 Sunday

_____
_____
_____
_____
_____
_____
_____
_____
_____
_____
_____

Wk	M	T	W	T	F	S	S
13							1
14	2	3	4	5	6	7	8
15	9	10	11	12	13	14	15
16	16	17	18	19	20	21	22
17	23	24	25	26	27	28	29
18	30						

April

9 Monday

Vimy Ridge Day (Can)

10 Tuesday

11 Wednesday

Yom HaShoah begins at sunset

April

2 Thursday

13 Friday

14 Saturday

15 Sunday

Wk	M	T	W	T	F	S	S
13							1
14	2	3	4	5	6	7	8
15	9	10	11	12	13	14	15
16	16	17	18	19	20	21	22
17	23	24	25	26	27	28	29
18	30						

April

16 Monday

Emancipation Day

17 Tuesday

18 Wednesday

April

19 Thursday

20 Friday

21 Saturday

22 Sunday

Wk	M	T	W	T	F	S	S
13							1
14	2	3	4	5	6	7	8
15	9	10	11	12	13	14	15
16	16	17	18	19	20	21	22
17	23	24	25	26	27	28	29
18	30						

April

23 Monday

St. George's Day

24 Tuesday

25 Wednesday

Anzac Day

April

26 Thursday

_____
_____
_____
_____
_____
_____
_____
_____
_____
_____
_____
_____
_____
_____
_____
_____
_____
_____
_____
_____
_____
_____
_____
_____
_____
_____

27 Friday

_____
_____
_____
_____
_____
_____
_____
_____
_____
_____
_____
_____
_____
_____
_____
_____
_____
_____
_____
_____
_____
_____
_____
_____

28 Saturday

_____
_____
_____
_____
_____
_____
_____

29 Sunday

_____
_____
_____
_____
_____
_____
_____
_____
_____
_____
_____

Wk	M	T	W	T	F	S	S
13							1
14	2	3	4	5	6	7	8
15	9	10	11	12	13	14	15
16	16	17	18	19	20	21	22
17	23	24	25	26	27	28	29
18	30						

HEN and JOE'S SPORTS TEASERS

Part One

We'll gie ye a choice for this first set o' questions. If ye get them a' richt, ye've been watchin' o'er much sport – like us!

1. **Wha has scored the maist Scottish League goals between:**
   a. Henrik Larsson
   b. John Robertson
   c. Ally McCoist

2. **Wha has won the maist Ryder Cup points between:**
   a. Colin Montgomerie
   b. Bernhard Langer
   c. Nick Faldo

3. **Wha has scored maist tries for Scotland between:**
   a. Tony Stanger
   b. Gavin Hastings
   c. Chris Paterson

There are mair questions in October and then a' the answers at the end!

May

A pyramid o' Broons so tall.
It's true, I'm no' a blether.
But they are headin' for a Fall –
They're knocked doon by a feather!

April / May

30 Monday

_____
_____
_____
_____
_____
_____
_____
_____
_____
_____
_____
_____
_____
_____
_____
_____
_____
_____
_____
_____
_____
_____
_____
_____

1 Tuesday

May Day
_____
_____
_____
_____
_____
_____
_____
_____
_____
_____
_____
_____
_____
_____
_____
_____
_____
_____
_____
_____
_____
_____
_____
_____

2 Wednesday

_____
_____
_____
_____
_____
_____
_____
_____
_____
_____
_____
_____
_____
_____
_____
_____
_____
_____
_____
_____
_____
_____
_____
_____

May

3 Thursday

4 Friday

5 Saturday

6 Sunday

Wk	M	T	W	T	F	S	S
18		1	2	3	4	5	6
19	7	8	9	10	11	12	13
20	14	15	16	17	18	19	20
21	21	22	23	24	25	26	27
22	28	29	30	31			

May

7 Monday

8 Tuesday

9 Wednesday

May

10 Thursday

...cension Day

_____

_____

_____

_____

_____

_____

_____

_____

_____

_____

_____

_____

_____

_____

_____

_____

_____

_____

_____

_____

11 Friday

_____

_____

_____

_____

_____

_____

_____

_____

_____

_____

_____

_____

_____

_____

_____

_____

_____

_____

_____

_____

12 Saturday

_____

_____

_____

_____

_____

_____

_____

13 Sunday

Mother's Day (Aus, Can, NZ, US)

_____

_____

_____

_____

_____

_____

_____

_____

_____

_____

Wk	M	T	W	T	F	S	S
18		1	2	3	4	5	6
19	7	8	9	10	11	12	13
20	14	15	16	17	18	19	20
21	21	22	23	24	25	26	27
22	28	29	30	31			

May

14 Monday

15 Tuesday

Ramadan begins at sunset

16 Wednesday

May

17 Thursday

_____
_____
_____
_____
_____
_____
_____
_____
_____
_____
_____
_____
_____
_____
_____
_____
_____
_____
_____
_____
_____
_____
_____
_____

18 Friday

_____
_____
_____
_____
_____
_____
_____
_____
_____
_____
_____
_____
_____
_____
_____
_____
_____
_____
_____
_____
_____
_____
_____
_____

19 Saturday

Shavuot begins at sunset
_____
_____
_____
_____
_____
_____
_____
_____

20 Sunday

Pentecost
_____
_____
_____
_____
_____
_____
_____
_____
_____

Wk	M	T	W	T	F	S	S
18		1	2	3	4	5	6
19	7	8	9	10	11	12	13
20	14	15	16	17	18	19	20
21	21	22	23	24	25	26	27
22	28	29	30	31			

May

21 Monday

Victoria Day

Shavuot ends at sunset

22 Tuesday

23 Wednesday

May

24 Thursday

25 Friday

26 Saturday

National Sorry Day (Aus)

27 Sunday

Trinity Sunday

Wk	M	T	W	T	F	S	S
18		1	2	3	4	5	6
19	7	8	9	10	11	12	13
20	14	15	16	17	18	19	20
21	21	22	23	24	25	26	27
22	28	29	30	31			

May

28 Monday

Spring Bank Holiday (UK, R of I)

Memorial Day (US)

29 Tuesday

30 Wednesday

June

A summer sea trip on a boat
Maks a' the Broons feel queasy.
Except for Gran'paw – see him gloat.
His rocker maks things easy!

THE BROONS

5/-

D. C. THOMSON & CO., LTD. GLASGOW — LONDON — DUNDEE

May / June

31 Thursday

ous Christi

_____

_____

_____

_____

_____

_____

_____

_____

_____

_____

_____

_____

_____

_____

_____

_____

_____

_____

_____

_____

_____

_____

1 Friday

_____

_____

_____

_____

_____

_____

_____

_____

_____

_____

_____

_____

_____

_____

_____

_____

_____

_____

_____

_____

_____

2 Saturday

_____

_____

_____

_____

_____

_____

_____

_____

_____

3 Sunday

_____

_____

_____

_____

_____

_____

_____

_____

_____

_____

Wk	M	T	W	T	F	S	S
22					1	2	3
23	4	5	6	7	8	9	10
24	11	12	13	14	15	16	17
25	18	19	20	21	22	23	24
26	25	26	27	28	29	30	

June

4 Monday

5 Tuesday

6 Wednesday

June

7 Thursday

8 Friday

9 Saturday

10 Sunday

Laylat al-Qadr begins at sunset

Wk	M	T	W	T	F	S	S
22					1	2	3
23	4	5	6	7	8	9	10
24	11	12	13	14	15	16	17
25	18	19	20	21	22	23	24
26	25	26	27	28	29	30	

June

11 Monday

12 Tuesday

13 Wednesday

June

14 Thursday

~~madan~~ ends at sunset

al-Fitr begins at sunset

15 Friday

16 Saturday

17 Sunday

Father's Day (UK, US, Can, R of I)

Wk	M	T	W	T	F	S	S
22					1	2	3
23	4	5	6	7	8	9	10
24	11	12	13	14	15	16	17
25	18	19	20	21	22	23	24
26	25	26	27	28	29	30	

June

18 Monday

19 Tuesday

20 Wednesday

June

21 Thursday

ummer Solstice

ational Aboriginal Day (Can)

22 Friday

23 Saturday

24 Sunday

St. John the Baptist Day

Wk	M	T	W	T	F	S	S
22					1	2	3
23	4	5	6	7	8	9	10
24	11	12	13	14	15	16	17
25	18	19	20	21	22	23	24
26	25	26	27	28	29	30	

June

25 Monday

26 Tuesday

27 Wednesday

July

Some Broons fowk head aff tae the sun.
A hoachin' beach's nae pleasure.
But twa auld guys are haein' fun -
They sunbathe at their leisure.

HORACE'S HEID
SCRATCHERS

1. Whit five-letter word looks just the same upside doon? Clue: The Bairn's goldfish does it.

2. Hen walks intae a pub and says tae the barman "Can I hae a glass o' water?" The barman pulls oot a shotgun from under the counter and points it at Hen. Hen says "Thanks, pal!" and walks oot o' the bar. Why?

3. Whit has fower hands (sometimes five) and is normal?

4. Whit word does this mean?

   AM^{U}OUS

   Clue: There could be more than one answer!!

5. Whit game is this?

   IS IS IS IS IS IS IS IS IS IS

6. Whit's Maw suffering from?

HEADACHE

Answers at the end!

June / July

28 Thursday

29 Friday

30 Saturday

1 Sunday

Canada Day

Wk	M	T	W	T	F	S	S
26							1
27	2	3	4	5	6	7	8
28	9	10	11	12	13	14	15
29	16	17	18	19	20	21	22
30	23	24	25	26	27	28	29
31	30	31					

July

2 Monday

3 Tuesday

4 Wednesday

Independence Day

July

5 Thursday

_____
_____
_____
_____
_____
_____
_____
_____
_____
_____
_____
_____
_____
_____
_____
_____
_____
_____
_____
_____
_____
_____
_____
_____
_____
_____

6 Friday

_____
_____
_____
_____
_____
_____
_____
_____
_____
_____
_____
_____
_____
_____
_____
_____
_____
_____
_____
_____
_____
_____
_____
_____
_____

7 Saturday

_____
_____
_____
_____
_____
_____
_____
_____
_____

8 Sunday

_____
_____
_____
_____
_____
_____
_____
_____
_____
_____
_____
_____
_____

Wk	M	T	W	T	F	S	S
26							1
27	2	3	4	5	6	7	8
28	9	10	11	12	13	14	15
29	16	17	18	19	20	21	22
30	23	24	25	26	27	28	29
31	30	31					

July

9 Monday

10 Tuesday

11 Wednesday

July

2 Thursday

...le of the Boyne

13 Friday

14 Saturday

15 Sunday

St. Swithin's Day

Wk	M	T	W	T	F	S	S
26							1
27	2	3	4	5	6	7	8
28	9	10	11	12	13	14	15
29	16	17	18	19	20	21	22
30	23	24	25	26	27	28	29
31	30	31					

July

16 Monday

17 Tuesday

18 Wednesday

July

9 Thursday

20 Friday

21 Saturday

Tisha B'Av begins at sunset

22 Sunday

Wk	M	T	W	T	F	S	S
26							1
27	2	3	4	5	6	7	8
28	9	10	11	12	13	14	15
29	16	17	18	19	20	21	22
30	23	24	25	26	27	28	29
31	30	31					

July

23 Monday

24 Tuesday

25 Wednesday

July

26 Thursday

_____
_____
_____
_____
_____
_____
_____
_____
_____
_____
_____
_____
_____
_____
_____
_____
_____
_____
_____
_____
_____
_____
_____
_____
_____

27 Friday

_____
_____
_____
_____
_____
_____
_____
_____
_____
_____
_____
_____
_____
_____
_____
_____
_____
_____
_____
_____
_____
_____

28 Saturday

_____
_____
_____
_____
_____
_____
_____

29 Sunday

_____
_____
_____
_____
_____
_____
_____
_____
_____
_____
_____

Wk	M	T	W	T	F	S	S
26							1
27	2	3	4	5	6	7	8
28	9	10	11	12	13	14	15
29	16	17	18	19	20	21	22
30	23	24	25	26	27	28	29
31	30	31					

ELEVEN BRAW BROONS

To the tune of "Three Blind Mice".

Eleven braw Broons . . .
Eleven braw Broons . . .
Did ever ye see such a family tree
For laughter—an' sometimes a tear in your e'e?
They're a' true to life, for they're just YOU an' ME!
Eleven Braw Broons.

Gran'paw's gettin' on . . .
Gran'paw's gettin' on . . .
He's the Broon that was in at the start.
They may come mair handsome, but never as smart!
The secret, of course, is he's still young in heart.
Gran'paw's getting on.

Good old Hen and Joe . . .
Good old Hen and Joe . . .
They're both Paw Broon's sons, yet they're like chalk and cheese.
It takes Joe a' his time to reach up to Hen's knees!
It's left to the TWINS to be like as twa peas.
Good old Hen and Joe.

Horace an' the Bairn . . .
Horace an' the Bairn—
Most likely to go far of a' the crew.
One o' them has enough brains for two—
And butter wouldna melt in the other yin's mou'!
Horace an' the Bairn

Bonnie Maggie Broon . . .
Bonnie Maggie Broon . . .
She's as sweet as the rose clingin' to the wa'
An' she is the fairest o' them a'—
"She gets it a' frae her feyther!" smirks Paw.
Bonnie Maggie Broon.

Daphne is a laugh . . .
Daphne is a laugh . . .
She's looked for Romance forty years or mair,
An' never progressed past the foot o' the stair!
But she "clicks" wi' us, so we shouldna care.
Daphne is the lass.

Then we come to Maw . . .
Then we come to Maw . . .
If teethache strikes in the middle o' the nig
If judgment is needed to settle a fight—
If a' this dreary old world needs put right—
THEN WE COME TO MAW!

August

Fitba' will soon be on the go.
Here comes anither season.
Auld Gran'paw playin' – surely no'!
But wait, here is the reason.

July / August

30 Monday

31 Tuesday

1 Wednesday

August

2 Thursday

3 Friday

4 Saturday

5 Sunday

Wk	M	T	W	T	F	S	S
31			1	2	3	4	5
32	6	7	8	9	10	11	12
33	13	14	15	16	17	18	19
34	20	21	22	23	24	25	26
35	27	28	29	30	31		

August

6 Monday

Civic Day (Can)

7 Tuesday

8 Wednesday

August

9 Thursday

_____
_____
_____
_____
_____
_____
_____
_____
_____
_____
_____
_____
_____
_____
_____
_____
_____
_____
_____
_____
_____
_____
_____

10 Friday

_____
_____
_____
_____
_____
_____
_____
_____
_____
_____
_____
_____
_____
_____
_____
_____
_____
_____
_____
_____

11 Saturday

_____
_____
_____
_____
_____
_____
_____
_____
_____

12 Sunday

_____
_____
_____
_____
_____
_____
_____
_____
_____

Wk	M	T	W	T	F	S	S
31			1	2	3	4	5
32	6	7	8	9	10	11	12
33	13	14	15	16	17	18	19
34	20	21	22	23	24	25	26
35	27	28	29	30	31		

August

13 Monday

14 Tuesday

15 Wednesday

August

16 Thursday

17 Friday

18 Saturday

19 Sunday

Wk	M	T	W	T	F	S	S
31		1	2	3	4	5	
32	6	7	8	9	10	11	12
33	13	14	15	16	17	18	19
34	20	21	22	23	24	25	26
35	27	28	29	30	31		

August

20 Monday

21 Tuesday

Eid al-Adha begins at sunset

22 Wednesday

August

23 Thursday

24 Friday

25 Saturday

Eid al-Adha ends at sunset

26 Sunday

Wk	M	T	W	T	F	S	S
31			1	2	3	4	5
32	6	7	8	9	10	11	12
33	13	14	15	16	17	18	19
34	20	21	22	23	24	25	26
35	27	28	29	30	31		

August

27 Monday

Summer Bank Holiday (UK)

28 Tuesday

29 Wednesday

September

Eighty candles – whit a price! –
For Gran'paw's big occasion.
Twa wee light bulbs are jist as nice
And saves much exhalation!

SCOTTISH INVENTIONS

THE TELEVISION – first demonstrated in 1926 by Helensburgh inventor John Logie Baird (1888–1946).

August / September

30 Thursday

31 Friday

1 Saturday

2 Sunday

Krishna Janmashtami

Father's Day (Aus, NZ)

Wk	M	T	W	T	F	S	S
35						1	2
36	3	4	5	6	7	8	9
37	10	11	12	13	14	15	16
38	17	18	19	20	21	22	23
39	24	25	26	27	28	29	30

September

3 Monday

Labor Day (US)

4 Tuesday

5 Wednesday

September

6 Thursday

7 Friday

8 Saturday

9 Sunday

Rosh Hashanah begins at sunset

Wk	M	T	W	T	F	S	S
35						1	2
36	3	4	5	6	7	8	9
37	10	11	12	13	14	15	16
38	17	18	19	20	21	22	23
39	24	25	26	27	28	29	30

September

10 Monday

Muharram begins at sunset

_____
_____
_____
_____
_____
_____
_____
_____
_____
_____
_____
_____
_____
_____
_____
_____
_____
_____
_____
_____
_____
_____
_____

11 Tuesday

Rosh Hashanah ends at sunset

_____
_____
_____
_____
_____
_____
_____
_____
_____
_____
_____
_____
_____
_____
_____
_____
_____
_____
_____
_____
_____
_____
_____

12 Wednesday

Ganesh Chaturthi begins

_____
_____
_____
_____
_____
_____
_____
_____
_____
_____
_____
_____
_____
_____
_____
_____
_____
_____
_____
_____
_____
_____
_____

September

13 Thursday

14 Friday

15 Saturday

16 Sunday

Wk	M	T	W	T	F	S	S
35						1	2
36	3	4	5	6	7	8	9
37	10	11	12	13	14	15	16
38	17	18	19	20	21	22	23
39	24	25	26	27	28	29	30

September

17 Monday

18 Tuesday

Yom Kippur begins at sunset

19 Wednesday

September

20 Thursday

_____
_____
_____
_____
_____
_____
_____
_____
_____
_____
_____
_____
_____
_____
_____
_____
_____
_____
_____
_____
_____
_____
_____
_____
_____

21 Friday

International Day of Peace (United Nations)

_____
_____
_____
_____
_____
_____
_____
_____
_____
_____
_____
_____
_____
_____
_____
_____
_____
_____
_____
_____
_____
_____
_____

22 Saturday

_____
_____
_____
_____
_____
_____
_____
_____
_____

23 Sunday

Ganesh Chaturthi ends

Sukkot begins at sunset

_____
_____
_____
_____
_____
_____
_____
_____
_____
_____
_____

Wk	M	T	W	T	F	S	S
35						1	2
36	3	4	5	6	7	8	9
37	10	11	12	13	14	15	16
38	17	18	19	20	21	22	23
39	24	25	26	27	28	29	30

September

24 Monday

25 Tuesday

26 Wednesday

September

27 Thursday

28 Friday

29 Saturday

30 Sunday

New Zealand Daylight Saving Time begins

Sukkot ends at sunset

Wk	M	T	W	T	F	S	S
35						1	2
36	3	4	5	6	7	8	9
37	10	11	12	13	14	15	16
38	17	18	19	20	21	22	23
39	24	25	26	27	28	29	30

HEN and JOE'S SPORTS TEASERS

Part Two

In this set o' questions, ye've got tae fill in the blanks.

These are harder than Gran'paw's pepperies!

4. Open championship venues in Scotland
a. 2018 Carnoustie   c. 2015 St Andrews
b. 2016 _____   d. 2013 Muirfield

5. Scottish winter olympic curling medalists 2014
a. Claire Hamilton   c. Anna Sloan
b. Vicki Adams   d. _____

6. Scottish BBC personality of the year winners
a. 2016 Andy Murray (and 2015 and 2013!)
b. 2008 Chris Hoy
c. 1991 _____
d. 1973 Jackie Stewart

Find oot if ye're right at the end o' the diary!

October

Paw and Gran'paw in the drink –
They're no' so happy lookin'.
O'er auld for games like this, ye'd think.
They've baith gone apple dookin'!

October

1 Monday

2 Tuesday

3 Wednesday

October

4 Thursday

5 Friday

6 Saturday

7 Sunday

Australian Daylight Saving Time begins

Wk	M	T	W	T	F	S	S
40	1	2	3	4	5	6	7
41	8	9	10	11	12	13	14
42	15	16	17	18	19	20	21
43	22	23	24	25	26	27	28
44	29	30	31				

October

8 Monday

Columbus Day (US))

9 Tuesday

Muharram ends at sunset

Navratri begins

10 Wednesday

World Porridge Day

October

1 Thursday

_____
_____
_____
_____
_____
_____
_____
_____
_____
_____
_____
_____
_____
_____
_____
_____
_____
_____
_____
_____
_____
_____
_____
_____

12 Friday

_____
_____
_____
_____
_____
_____
_____
_____
_____
_____
_____
_____
_____
_____
_____
_____
_____
_____
_____
_____
_____
_____
_____
_____

13 Saturday

_____
_____
_____
_____
_____
_____
_____
_____

14 Sunday

_____
_____
_____
_____
_____
_____
_____
_____
_____
_____
_____
_____

Wk	M	T	W	T	F	S	S
40	1	2	3	4	5	6	7
41	8	9	10	11	12	13	14
42	15	16	17	18	19	20	21
43	22	23	24	25	26	27	28
44	29	30	31				

October

15 Monday

16 Tuesday

17 Wednesday

Navratri ends

October

18 Thursday

19 Friday

20 Saturday

21 Sunday

Wk	M	T	W	T	F	S	S
40	1	2	3	4	5	6	7
41	8	9	10	11	12	13	14
42	15	16	17	18	19	20	21
43	22	23	24	25	26	27	28
44	29	30	31				

October

22 Monday

23 Tuesday

24 Wednesday

October

25 Thursday

26 Friday

27 Saturday

28 Sunday

British Summer Time ends

Wk	M	T	W	T	F	S	S
40	1	2	3	4	5	6	7
41	8	9	10	11	12	13	14
42	15	16	17	18	19	20	21
43	22	23	24	25	26	27	28
44	29	30	31				

October

29 Monday

30 Tuesday

31 Wednesday

Halloween

November

It sure is Baltic in the park –
The weather has been dire.
Says Gran'paw "Stuff this fur a lark –
Let's sit beside the fire!"

SCOTTISH INVENTIONS

THE BICYCLE – a mainly wooden version of which was demonstrated by Kirkpatrick Macmillan (1812–1878) from Keir in Dumfries and Galloway.

November

1 Thursday
All Saints' Day

2 Friday
All Souls' Day

3 Saturday

4 Sunday
Daylight Saving Time ends (US, Can)

Wk	M	T	W	T	F	S	S
44				1	2	3	4
45	5	6	7	8	9	10	11
46	12	13	14	15	16	17	18
47	19	20	21	22	23	24	25
48	26	27	28	29	30		

November

5 Monday

Guy Fawkes Night (UK)

6 Tuesday

7 Wednesday

Diwali begins

November

8 Thursday

9 Friday

10 Saturday

11 Sunday

Remembrance Sunday (UK)

Veterans Day (US)

Diwali ends

Wk	M	T	W	T	F	S	S
44				1	2	3	4
45	5	6	7	8	9	10	11
46	12	13	14	15	16	17	18
47	19	20	21	22	23	24	25
48	26	27	28	29	30		

November

12 Monday

_____
_____
_____
_____
_____
_____
_____
_____
_____
_____
_____
_____
_____
_____
_____
_____
_____
_____
_____
_____

13 Tuesday

Robert Louis Stevenson Day

_____
_____
_____
_____
_____
_____
_____
_____
_____
_____
_____
_____
_____
_____
_____
_____
_____
_____
_____
_____

14 Wednesday

_____
_____
_____
_____
_____
_____
_____
_____
_____
_____
_____
_____
_____
_____
_____
_____
_____
_____
_____
_____

November

15 Thursday

16 Friday

17 Saturday

18 Sunday

Wk	M	T	W	T	F	S	S
44				1	2	3	4
45	5	6	7	8	9	10	11
46	12	13	14	15	16	17	18
47	19	20	21	22	23	24	25
48	26	27	28	29	30		

November

19 Monday

20 Tuesday

21 Wednesday

November

22 Thursday

anksgiving Day (US)

23 Friday

24 Saturday

25 Sunday

Wk	M	T	W	T	F	S	S
44				1	2	3	4
45	5	6	7	8	9	10	11
46	12	13	14	15	16	17	18
47	19	20	21	22	23	24	25
48	26	27	28	29	30		

November

26 Monday

27 Tuesday

28 Wednesday

December

Tae Prannie Pond the Broons head doon.
At skatin' they're a' rookies.
They a' regret their trip quite soon,
As they've a' got bruised bahookies.

St Andrew's Day Shortie

Mary Berry wid gie her eye teeth for these!

YE'LL NEED:
8 oz/225 g butter
8 oz/225 g plain flour
4 oz/110 g cornflour
4 oz/110 g icing sugar

METHOD:
Pre-heat yer oven tae 150 degrees.

1. Combine the butter and icing sugar the gither until the mixture's braw and smooth.
2. Add the plain flour and cornflour and mix it till ye form a dough.
3. Roll oot the dough till it's aboot 1cm thick.
4. Using a cake cutter, cut intae shapes.
5. Place on a baking tray and bake in yer oven for aboot 45 minutes. Keep a guid eye on it though, cos cooking times can vary. When yer shorties are golden broon then they're ready.
6. Allow tae cool then watch them disappear doon the family's throats.

November / December

9 Thursday

_____
_____
_____
_____
_____
_____
_____
_____
_____
_____
_____
_____
_____
_____
_____
_____
_____
_____
_____
_____
_____
_____
_____
_____

30 Friday

St. Andrew's Day

_____
_____
_____
_____
_____
_____
_____
_____
_____
_____
_____
_____
_____
_____
_____
_____
_____
_____
_____
_____
_____
_____

1 Saturday

_____
_____
_____
_____
_____
_____
_____
_____
_____

2 Sunday

Advent Sunday

Hanukkah begins at sunset

Wk	M	T	W	T	F	S	S
48						1	2
49	3	4	5	6	7	8	9
50	10	11	12	13	14	15	16
51	17	18	19	20	21	22	23
52	24	25	26	27	28	29	30
53	31						

December

3 Monday

4 Tuesday

5 Wednesday

December

6 Thursday

_____
_____
_____
_____
_____
_____
_____
_____
_____
_____
_____
_____
_____
_____
_____
_____
_____
_____
_____
_____
_____
_____
_____
_____

7 Friday

_____
_____
_____
_____
_____
_____
_____
_____
_____
_____
_____
_____
_____
_____
_____
_____
_____
_____
_____
_____
_____
_____
_____
_____

8 Saturday

_____
_____
_____
_____
_____
_____
_____
_____

9 Sunday

_____
_____
_____
_____
_____
_____
_____
_____
_____

Wk	M	T	W	T	F	S	S
48						1	2
49	3	4	5	6	7	8	9
50	10	11	12	13	14	15	16
51	17	18	19	20	21	22	23
52	24	25	26	27	28	29	30
53	31						

December

10 Monday

Human Rights Day

Hanukkah ends at sunset

11 Tuesday

12 Wednesday

December

13 Thursday

14 Friday

15 Saturday

16 Sunday

Wk	M	T	W	T	F	S	S
48						1	2
49	3	4	5	6	7	8	9
50	10	11	12	13	14	15	16
51	17	18	19	20	21	22	23
52	24	25	26	27	28	29	30
53	31						

December

17 Monday

Anniversary of Statute of Westminster (Can)

18 Tuesday

19 Wednesday

December

20 Thursday

21 Friday

Winter Solstice

22 Saturday

23 Sunday

Wk	M	T	W	T	F	S	S
48						1	2
49	3	4	5	6	7	8	9
50	10	11	12	13	14	15	16
51	17	18	19	20	21	22	23
52	24	25	26	27	28	29	30
53	31						

December

24 Monday

Christmas Eve

_____
_____
_____
_____
_____
_____
_____
_____
_____
_____
_____
_____
_____
_____
_____
_____
_____
_____
_____
_____
_____
_____
_____
_____
_____
_____

25 Tuesday

Christmas Day, holiday

_____
_____
_____
_____
_____
_____
_____
_____
_____
_____
_____
_____
_____
_____
_____
_____
_____
_____
_____
_____
_____
_____
_____
_____
_____
_____

26 Wednesday

Boxing Day, holiday

_____
_____
_____
_____
_____
_____
_____
_____
_____
_____
_____
_____
_____
_____
_____
_____
_____
_____
_____
_____
_____
_____
_____
_____
_____
_____

December

27 Thursday

28 Friday

29 Saturday

30 Sunday

Wk	M	T	W	T	F	S	S
48						1	2
49	3	4	5	6	7	8	9
50	10	11	12	13	14	15	16
51	17	18	19	20	21	22	23
52	24	25	26	27	28	29	30
53	31						

December / January

31 Monday

Hogmanay (New Year's Eve)

1 Tuesday

New Year's Day, holiday

2 Wednesday

Holiday (Scot)

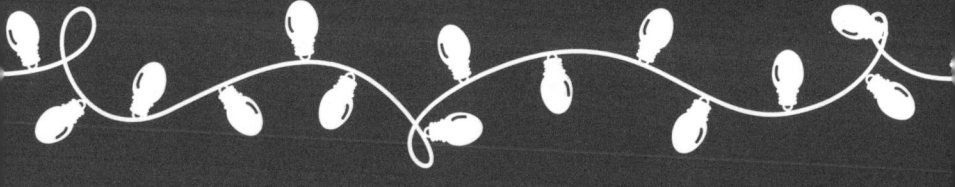

Merry Christmas and Happy New Year from the Broons!

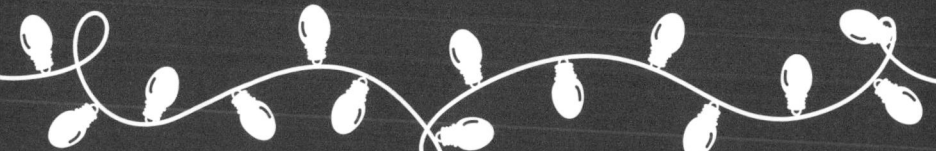

HEN and JOE'S SPORTS TEASERS

Answers

1. Oot o' the three, Ally McCoist has scored the maist Scottish League goals with 282. John Robertson scored 229 and Henrik Larsson got 174. But ony o' them are welcome tae join oor Sunday team onytime!

2. Nick Faldo won the maist Ryder Cup points with 25, closely followed by Berhard Langer on 24 and Colin Montgomery on 23.5.

3. Tony Stanger came oot on top wi' 24 tries for Scotland, while Chris Paterson got 22 and Gavin Hastings got 17.

4. The Open was held in Troon in 2016.

5. The ither curling medallist was Eve Muirhead.

6. Liz McColgan was the BBC Sports Personality of the Year in 1991.

How did ye dae? If ye got them a' right, we want you on oor pub quiz team!

Horace's Heid Scratchers

Answers

1. SWIMS

2. Hen wanted the water for his hiccups but the fright from the gun did the trick just as well

3. A man wi' a wristwatch (five hands if the watch has a second hand)

4. AMBIGUOUS

5. TENNIS

6. A splittin' headache

Notes

Notes

Notes

....

....

....

....

....

....

....

....

....

....

....

....

....

....

....

Notes

....

....

....

....

....

....

....

....

....

....

....

....

....

....

First published 2017
by Black & White Publishing Ltd
29 Ocean Drive, Edinburgh EH6 6JL

ISBN: 978 1 910230 40 4

A CIP catalogue record for this book is available from the British Library.

Printed and bound by Opolgraf, Poland